Jackie (2023 Revised and Analyzed)

ISBN 978-1-312-23919-7

Zachariah Oliver
Copyright@2023

TABLE OF CONTENT

CHAPTER 1 3

   INTRODUCTION 3

CHAPTER 2 10

   Early Life and Education 10

CHAPTER 3 15

   Marriage to John F. Kennedy 15

CHAPTER 4 22

   Cultural and Fashion Icon 22

CHAPTER 5 28

   Preservation of Historic Legacy 28

CHAPTER 6 33

   Tragic Events and Later Life 33

CHAPTER 7 40

   Philanthropic Activities 40

THE END 45

CHAPTER 1

INTRODUCTION

Jacqueline Bouvier Kennedy Onassis, also known as Jackie Kennedy, is a prominent and influential woman in American history, renowned for her significant contributions to culture, fashion, and the political sphere. Jackie was born on July 28, 1929, into a family of high social standing in Southampton, New York. Her life trajectory would later evolve into a compelling narrative characterized by grace, fortitude, misfortune, and perseverance. The impact she exerted beyond her position as the First Lady of the United States, profoundly altering the cultural milieu of her time and serving as a lasting source of inspiration for subsequent generations.

The life of Jacqueline Kennedy Onassis was characterized by a rich tapestry interwoven with elements of affluence and refinement. The father of the individual in question, John "Black Jack" Bouvier III, had significant fortune as a stockbroker. Conversely, the mother, Janet Norton Lee Bouvier Auchincloss, was from a well-established family with connections to the upper echelons of society. The individual's upbringing not only provided her with exposure to refined elements of existence, but also cultivated within her a profound commitment and obligation towards the global community.

From an early stage in her development, Jackie had an exceptional cognitive capacity and a strong inclination towards artistic pursuits. The individual in question received her education from prestigious academic establishments, such as Miss Porter's School located in Connecticut, and thereafter pursued her studies at Vassar College. During this developmental period, her enthusiasm for literature, journalism, and the humanities was nurtured, establishing the groundwork for her subsequent endeavors. It was during her tenure at Vassar College that she developed a profound admiration for literature and a discerning acuity for meticulousness, attributes that would significantly shape her subsequent experiences.

The pivotal phase in Jackie's life started with her encounter with John F. Kennedy, a captivating and influential senator hailing from Massachusetts. The process of their romantic relationship was characterized by a rapid and intense pace, distinguished by a mutual intellectual bond and a reciprocal intrigue in each other's personal experiences. The matrimonial union of the pair in 1953 denoted the convergence of two prominent lineages and served as a symbolic indication of their initiation into the realm of politics. Unbeknownst to Jackie, her position as the spouse of John F. Kennedy would propel her into the worldwide platform, resulting in her metamorphosis into a symbol of elegance and a renowned figure of fashion during a period marked by significant upheaval.

The period during which Jackie Kennedy served as the First Lady of the United States, spanning from 1961 to 1963, brought about significant redefinitions to the position that have had a lasting impact. Her presence in the White House introduced a renewed sense of cultural refinement and elegance, infusing the environment with a refreshing and invigorating ambiance. The influence of Jackie on the fashion industry was especially remarkable. Her sophisticated and polished sense of style established new fashion trends that reverberated across society, resulting in her being affectionately referred to as "Jackie O." The fashion selections made by the individual in question were distinguished by their uncomplicated designs, vivid hues, and the use of pillbox caps. These choices were extensively emulated and solidified her position as a prominent influencer of contemporary fashion trends.

In addition to her notable fashion sense, Jackie used her influential position to advocate for the advancement of American arts and culture. The individual in question spearheaded the establishment of the White House Historical Association, with a primary objective of safeguarding and upholding the historical importance of the presidential abode. The individual's passion for artistic endeavors was clearly shown via her endeavors to meticulously restore the White House to its previous magnificence. In this pursuit, she actively sought the assistance of knowledgeable specialists and curators to guarantee the preservation of its historical authenticity.

Nevertheless, a significant shift occurred on November 22, 1963, when President Kennedy was tragically slain in Dallas, Texas. The very distressing occurrence not only devastated Jackie's personal realm but also had a profound impact on the collective morale of the country. Amidst her profound sorrow, she exhibited exceptional poise and fortitude, guiding a bereaved nation by her dignified demeanor during her spouse's burial cortege. The demonstration of unwavering determination in the midst of indescribable adversity garnered her favor among the citizens of the United States, establishing her as an emblem of composure under challenging circumstances.

In the aftermath of the killing, Jackie Kennedy actively sought consolation and isolation. Subsequently, she entered into a marital union with Aristotle Onassis, a prominent Greek figure in the shipping industry. Although the marriage garnered much media coverage, it also signified a period of relative solitude for her. Following the death of Onassis, Jacqueline Kennedy Onassis returned to the United States and reignited her fervor for literature and the arts. She embarked upon a career in the publishing industry and achieved proficiency as an editor, gaining experience at many publishing establishments while showcasing her dedication to cultural endeavors.

Jackie's impact extends beyond her public persona and fashion sense. The humanitarian pursuits she engaged in served as evidence of her empathetic nature and unwavering commitment to effecting beneficial change. She demonstrated active engagement with esteemed institutions such as the Metropolitan Museum of Art and the Kennedy Center, where she played a pivotal role in advocating for the arts and contributing to educational endeavors. The individual's endeavors to protect and maintain significant historical sites, such as the meticulous refurbishment of the White House, served as a testament to her unwavering dedication to the preservation of the country's cultural legacy, ensuring its longevity for forthcoming cohorts.

In summary, the life narrative of Jackie Kennedy is characterized by a rich amalgamation of sophistication, fortitude, and impact. With regards to her wealthy upbringing and education, along with her influential position as a revolutionary First Lady, she undeniably had a lasting impact on American society. The individual's discernment in fashion, advocacy for cultural advancement, and unwavering commitment to safeguarding historical heritage persistently influence and motivate the broader community. In addition to her public persona, Jackie's adeptness in handling adversity with poise and her dedication to charitable endeavors exemplified her multidimensional nature. The ongoing significance of her legacy serves as a poignant reminder that, even in the midst of challenging circumstances, resilience and grace have the power to radiate, leaving an indelible imprint on society.

CHAPTER 2

Early Life and Education

Jacqueline Lee Bouvier, thereafter recognized as Jackie Kennedy, was born on July 28, 1929, into a milieu characterized by affluence and sophistication. The formative years of her life were characterized by the convergence of affluence, cultural exposure, and educational opportunities, so establishing the foundation for her subsequent eminence as a significant figure in both cultural and political spheres. Jacqueline Bouvier, also known as Jackie, was born to John "Black Jack" Bouvier III and Janet Norton Lee Bouvier Auchincloss. This familial background bestowed upon her a heritage that significantly influenced her perspectives and ambitions.

During her formative years in Southampton, New York, Jackie experienced a milieu characterized by affluence and refinement. The paternal figure, John Bouvier, had substantial fortune as a stockbroker and was renowned for his charm and extensive social networks. Conversely, the maternal figure, Janet Lee, hailed from a lineage well entrenched in societal circles. Jackie was exposed to a world of affluence and refinement due to the diverse backgrounds of her parents, which included many social events, galas, and cultural activities that constituted an intrinsic aspect of their everyday lives.

From an early age, it was evident that Jackie had a keen intelligence and an inherent inquisitiveness about her surroundings. The development of her inquisitiveness was fostered by her parents, who acknowledged her desire for intellectual growth and encouraged her to delve into several areas of study. During her early years, she shown a strong affinity for reading and writing, often immersing herself in the narratives of renowned literary works. The individual's early inclination towards reading not only augmented their lexical repertoire, but also served as the foundation for their subsequent inclination towards the realms of arts and journalism.

Jackie begun her academic trajectory at Miss Porter's School located in Farmington, Connecticut. The renowned educational school exclusively for female students was well recognized for its commitment to rigorous academic standards, fostering personal growth, and cultivating refinement.

It was in this context that Jackie's cognitive abilities fully thrived. The person demonstrated exceptional academic performance and wholeheartedly embraced the educational institution's philosophy of fostering people who possess a comprehensive skill set and a profound commitment to societal obligations.

During her tenure at Miss Porter's School, she was deeply immersed in the realm of the arts and humanities. Jackie's burgeoning fascination with literature and the visual arts started to manifest itself throughout her tenure at the educational institution. The individual actively engaged in theatrical performances, explored several avenues of creative expression, and had a refined sense of aesthetic appreciation. These formative experiences served as the basis for her subsequent position as a benefactor of the arts and a significant force in shaping cultural trends.

Following her graduation from Miss Porter's School, Jackie embarked on her educational journey at Vassar College, a renowned school renowned for its dedication to the advancement of women's education and intellectual emancipation. In this context, she consistently demonstrated exceptional academic performance and actively engaged with a dynamic academic environment. During her time at Vassar, she engaged in a more comprehensive exploration of her academic pursuits, focusing her study on French literature and refining her abilities in analytical reasoning and critical evaluation.

During her tenure at Vassar, Jackie had the opportunity to foster significant contacts and establish ties with her fellow students. The individual actively participated in intellectual discourse, engaging in debates, conversations, and partnerships that served to expand their viewpoints and enhance their comprehension of diverse topics. The academic experience at the university not only enhanced her passion for literature and the arts, but also cultivated a strong feeling of autonomy and self-confidence.

Jackie's burgeoning interest in journalism emerged throughout her collegiate tenure. The individual in question had positions as a photographer and writer for the Vassar Miscellany News, which is the student newspaper of the aforementioned institution. The first ventures into journalism provided her with the opportunity to merge her passion for writing with her developing admiration for photography, a fusion that would afterwards become a distinguishing characteristic of her public image.

In brief, the formative years and educational background of Jackie Kennedy were characterized by a convergence of advantageous circumstances, intellectual prowess, and exposure to many cultural experiences. Having been nurtured in an affluent and cultured milieu, she cultivated a profound inquisitiveness and a discerning admiration for the arts throughout her formative years. The individual's intellectual abilities were further developed and their involvement in literature, journalism, and the humanities was expanded via their educational experiences at esteemed schools such as Miss Porter's School and Vassar College. These early experiences established the foundation for her subsequent status as a cultural symbol, molding her into the individual whose grace, intelligence, and perseverance would attract global interest in the future.

CHAPTER 3

Marriage to John F. Kennedy

The matrimonial bond between Jacqueline Bouvier and John F. Kennedy might be seen as a partnership that beyond mere affection, evolving into an emblematic representation of optimism, elegance, and collective ambition on a national scale. The process of their courtship, marriage, and ensuing years of companionship would not only significantly influence their individual lives but also have a profound impact on the course of American history.
The narrative surrounding their marital union encapsulates a symbiotic relationship characterized by intellectual synergy, reciprocal assistance, and the resilience to withstand both moments of success and adversity.

The first encounter between Jackie and John occurred over a dinner gathering in the year 1951, initiating a bond that subsequently developed into a romantic relationship characterized by reciprocal admiration and intellectual affinity. During that period, John F. Kennedy, a dynamic and youthful politician, had already garnered widespread national recognition due to his exceptional oratory skills and forward-thinking ideas. Jackie, who had just completed her studies at Vassar College and was now employed as a photographer and writer, had an undeniable allure stemming from her physical attractiveness, composure, and intellectual acumen.

The courting between the individuals in question was characterized by a lack of ostentation or public displays. Instead, it was a process marked by the exploration of common interests and engaging talks, which served to strengthen their bond. The presence of intellectual stimulation between them was apparent, as they actively participated in conversations pertaining to literature, politics, and the prospective trajectory of the nation. The cognitive resonance established the basis for a love engagement that was also grounded in a mutual aspiration to effect positive change on a global scale.

The public's fascination was piqued in 1953 by their engagement, which symbolized the merging of two prominent families and signified the potential for transformative change. The nuptial ceremony, which took place on September 12, 1953, was a lavish occasion that exemplified the couple's refinement and elegance. The gown worn by Jackie, which was created by Ann Lowe, exhibited exceptional craftsmanship and artistry. It skillfully merged elements of heritage with contemporary aesthetics, so establishing a precedent for her influential position as a cultural innovator.

As John F. Kennedy's political trajectory progressed, Jackie's position as a supporting companion also advanced. Although her public image projected an air of sophistication and poise, she also shown a profound political astuteness in private. The individual in question had a comprehension of the significance associated with image and message, therefore contributing to the formation of her spouse's public image. This was accomplished by her fastidious dedication to careful attention to detail in several domains, including but not limited to décor, fashion, and social interactions.

Upon becoming the president in 1961, John F. Kennedy's wife, Jackie Kennedy, took the position of First Lady and embarked on a mission to include culture and art into the White House. The endeavors she pursued were not just concerned with aesthetics, but rather served as a manifestation of her conviction that art and culture are important elements for the prosperity of a community. The individual in question established the White House Historical Association, with a primary objective of preserving the historical authenticity of the presidential mansion, while also highlighting American art and tradition.

The impact of Jackie's tenure as First Lady on the fashion industry is of significant importance and should not be underestimated. The individual's exceptional fashion sense, distinguished by its sleek designs, vibrant hues, and sophisticated aesthetic, led to her being referred to as "Jackie O." The fashion selections made by her went beyond mere trends, ultimately shaping a specific period of time and establishing a lasting influence on the fashion landscape of the United States. The individual's admiration for European couture was effectively counterbalanced by her dedication to advancing the work of American designers, therefore achieving a harmonious equilibrium between international refinement and patriotic allegiance.

Nevertheless, the Kennedy administration had several difficulties. The couple encountered political upheaval, such as the Cuban Missile Crisis and the civil rights movement, which served as a means to assess their ability to endure and adapt. Notwithstanding these challenges, Jackie exhibited remarkable resilience, providing steadfast assistance to her spouse while portraying an air of composure that offered comfort to the American populace throughout periods of ambiguity.

The culmination of their collaborative alliance reached a sorrowful conclusion on November 22, 1963, when President Kennedy was subject to an assassination in Dallas, Texas. The very distressing occurrence deeply impacted the whole country and propelled Jackie into the position of a bereaved widow, whose poise and composure in the midst of overwhelming sadness left an enduring imprint on the annals of history. The global audience saw her procession with her spouse's coffin, displaying fortitude and perseverance despite her own anguish.

The American populace was profoundly moved by Jackie's remarkable ability to maneuver through immense grief with remarkable grace. The composure shown by the individual in question throughout those challenging instances not only provided solace to a grieving populace, but also established her as a lasting emblem of gracefulness in the face of adversity.

In summary, the marital union of Jacqueline Bouvier and John F. Kennedy may be characterized as a relationship that beyond mere personal affection, assuming a significant role in the annals of American history. The romance and relationship between the individuals were founded around a same intellectual bond and a shared aspiration to make constructive contributions to society. The role of Jackie as the First Lady brought forth a redefinition of the post, as she introduced elements of culture and elegance into the White House. Despite the many challenges encountered, which notably included the tragic event of President Kennedy's murder, Jackie's lasting elegance and resilience have established an indelible heritage that continues to serve as a source of inspiration for subsequent generations. The narrative presented by the individual serves as a poignant testament to the enduring impact of love, intellectual prowess, and unwavering determination on the course of historical events. It serves as a poignant reminder that these influential forces possess the capacity to leave an indelible mark that transcends the boundaries of time.

CHAPTER 4

Cultural and Fashion Icon

The enduring impact of Jackie Kennedy as a cultural and fashion symbol is unmatched, beyond temporal and geographical boundaries. The enduring influence of her contributions to style, elegance, and the arts resonates, solidifying her position as an emblem of poise and refinement. Jackie's enduring impact on global culture and style is evident in her calm manner and pioneering wardrobe choices.

The initiation of Jackie's public presence as the First Lady of the United States in 1961 signified the commencement of her evolution as a prominent figure in the realm of culture. From the outset, her inherent sense of style was readily apparent, garnering the interest of both the American populace and the global world. The individual's discerning preference and subtly sophisticated style provided a welcome break from the overtly extravagant fashions prevalent at that era.

One of the most noteworthy achievements made by Jackie was her adeptness in reconciling the dichotomy between traditional and modern fashion. The individual's sartorial selections, often distinguished by their minimalistic design, unadorned outlines, and flawless craftsmanship, demonstrated her admiration for enduring sophistication. The sunglasses famously associated with Jacqueline Kennedy Onassis, colloquially known as "Jackie O" sunglasses, gained recognition as a distinctive item and a notable fashion statement due to their large size, which served the purpose of providing her with protection from intrusive photographers.

Her impact reached beyond the realm of fashion and expanded into the domain of home design. In her capacity as the First Lady, she embarked upon the formidable endeavor of revitalizing the White House to its previous state of magnificence. Through her diligent efforts, she successfully conserved and accentuated the historical import of the presidential abode, therefore metamorphosing it into a vibrant repository of American history and cultural heritage. By means of painstaking restoration efforts and a keen focus on detail, she exemplified the potential of architecture and design as influential tools for the conservation of a nation's cultural legacy.

The influence of Jackie on the fashion industry was further linked to her advocacy for American designers and her capacity to foster a collective perception of national identity via her sartorial choices. The individual acknowledged the significance of her position in promoting the skills and abilities of American designers, so making a valuable contribution to the cultural and economic advancement of the nation. Through the use of garments crafted by renowned designers like as Oleg Cassini and Bill Blass, she effectively enhanced their prominence on an international scale, so contributing to the establishment of American fashion as a formidable presence in the industry.

The European excursions undertaken by the individual in question, namely her trip to France with President Kennedy, were used as opportunities to exhibit her cultivated aesthetic preferences and advance diplomatic objectives via the medium of fashion. The manner in which she engaged with prominent individuals, such as Yvonne de Gaulle, the First Lady of France, demonstrated her aptitude for fostering cross-cultural connections by means of her sartorial selections. The costumes she often wore were indicative of the cultural legacy of the nations she traveled through, demonstrating respect for indigenous customs while maintaining her distinctive fashion sense.

Jackie's cultural impact extended beyond the realm of fashion, as she shown a strong commitment to promoting the arts. The individual's profound appreciation for literature, music, and theater was clearly shown by her dedicated endeavors to elevate these cultural facets inside the American community. She converted the White House into a space for cultural events, extending invitations to artists, musicians, and authors to interact with political figures and intellectuals. The contributions made by her established the groundwork for the White House's ongoing function as a hub for cultural interchange.

The lasting impact of Jackie's cultural and sartorial influence may be attributed to her genuine personality and her capacity to establish meaningful connections with individuals at an intimate level. Notwithstanding her heightened social position, she was often seen as sympathetic and accessible, attributes that drew her to the general populace. The individual's sartorial selections had qualities of both inspiration and accessibility, making her a source of inspiration for women from many backgrounds who aspired to replicate her fashion sense.

In the subsequent years subsequent to her tenure as First Lady, Jackie's impact continued to reverberate. The persistent influence of designers and celebrities further strengthened her imprint on the fashion industry. The enduring impact of her contributions was perpetuated by designers who found inspiration in her outstanding fashion choices. The enduring impact of her influence is evident in the multitude of films, television shows, and documentaries that have delved into her life, distinctive fashion sense, and significant cultural achievements.

In conclusion, the cultural and fashion impact of Jackie Kennedy serves as a tribute to her distinctive combination of elegance, genuineness, and sophisticated aesthetic. The enduring influence she has had on fashion trends, home design, and the dissemination of American culture serves as a source of inspiration for designers, artists, and people throughout the globe. The individual's adeptness in traversing the convergence of style, culture, and diplomacy distinguished her as a forward-thinking figure whose impact endures throughout the ages. Jackie Kennedy's everlasting legacy serves as a poignant reminder that style encompasses more than just sartorial choices; it encompasses the capacity to influence culture and have a lasting impact on society.

CHAPTER 5

Preservation of Historic Legacy

The impact of Jackie Kennedy reaches beyond her renowned status as a fashion icon and First Lady, including her unwavering commitment to safeguarding the historical and cultural legacy of the United States. The individual's dedication to safeguarding historical sites and advancing American arts and culture has had a lasting impact on the nation's historical narrative, guaranteeing the maintenance of prior narratives for forthcoming cohorts.

During her tenure as First Lady, Jackie had a notable impact on historical preservation via her restoration efforts on the White House. Upon her arrival to the presidential mansion, she was immediately struck by the absence of historical authenticity seen in its interior design. Motivated by a strong will to reinstate the White House to its previous state of magnificence, she undertook an ambitious and scrupulous endeavor of restoration, with the objective of encapsulating the fundamental characteristics of several historical epochs.

Under Jackie's supervision, a thorough restoration endeavor was undertaken in collaboration with professionals, historians, and curators, resulting in the reinstatement of the White House's interior to its former splendor and adherence to historical authenticity. The individual included furniture, artwork, and décor that were suitable for the time period, so acknowledging and respecting the building's significant historical background, but also guaranteeing its relevance in the present day. The author's commitment to maintaining historical accuracy demonstrated her recognition of the significance of safeguarding the cultural legacy of the country.

Jackie's endeavors also included areas outside the confines of the White House. This endeavor emphasized her conviction that the White House served as more than simply a dwelling, but rather as an emblem of the country's historical legacy and principles. The organisation diligently undertook the task of methodically documenting and disseminating the tales of former presidents and their families to the general public.
Furthermore, Jackie's commitment to the preservation of historical sites extended beyond the confines of the White House. The individual demonstrated an awareness

of the significance associated with the conservation of other historical sites that had a vital role in shaping the overall narrative of American history. She advocated for programs aimed at preserving and revitalizing historical places, so guaranteeing their long-term accessibility for future generations. Her active participation in esteemed organizations such as the National Trust for Historic Preservation served as a testament to her unwavering dedication to the protection and preservation of the United States' architectural and cultural heritage.

Jackie's fervor for history was intricately linked with her admiration for the arts and culture. The individual had the belief that art has the capacity to transcend temporal boundaries and establish connections among individuals across different epochs. In order to foster the advancement of American culture, she organized gatherings in the White House that commemorated artistic expression and intellectual pursuits, extending invitations to artists, musicians, authors, and intellectuals to partake in meaningful cultural discourse. The individual's capacity to integrate cultural enrichment with diplomatic endeavors emphasized their distinct methodology in promoting global comprehension via artistic means.

Furthermore, her impact on the preservation of culture was especially evident in the field of education. Acknowledging the significance of fostering the cultivation of historical and cultural awareness among forthcoming generations, she campaigned for the integration of arts instruction inside educational institutions. The individual had the belief that through the cultivation of knowledge in history and the arts, young people might develop into well-informed members of society who possess a deep appreciation for the need of conserving historical heritage.

Jackie's dedication to the preservation of historical artifacts and the enrichment of cultural heritage extended beyond a mere personal interest. It served as a deep manifestation of her recognition of the significance of continuity and the valuable insights that can be gleaned from studying history. The endeavors she undertook provided evidence that the past is not a fixed and unchanging concept, but rather a dynamic and ongoing story that influences the current state of affairs and molds what lies ahead. Through the preservation of historic sites, relics, and narratives, she effectively maintained the preservation of the nation's identity, which remained firmly grounded in its extensive and varied past.

In summary, the commitment of Jackie Kennedy to the preservation of historical heritage serves as evidence of her many contributions to American culture. Through her careful and thorough efforts in restoring the White House, founding the White House Historical Association, and actively advocating for the preservation of historic monuments, she demonstrated a steadfast dedication to conserving the cultural legacy of the country. The individual's conviction in the capacity of arts and culture to surpass limitations serves as a notable demonstration of her exceptional aptitude in connecting historical contexts and diplomatic endeavors. By virtue of her deeds, she established a lasting heritage that perpetually instills a profound admiration for historical events and their significance in molding a more knowledgeable and interconnected future.

CHAPTER 6

Tragic Events and Later Life

The life trajectory of Jacqueline Kennedy Onassis was characterized by significant instances of great sorrow as well as extraordinary endurance. Jackie's resilience and composure in the midst of tragedy, starting with the profound loss of her spouse and continuing throughout following phases, served as a monument to her unwavering fortitude and adeptness in navigating the most arduous conditions that life presents.

The pivotal moment that would significantly influence the subsequent phase of Jackie's life occurred on the momentous day of November 22, 1963, when President John F. Kennedy was tragically slain in Dallas, Texas. The reverberations of this horrific incident extended beyond the borders of the United States, resonating globally. At the age of 34, Jackie was unexpectedly placed in the position of a bereaved widow, attracting global attention as she coped with an indescribable tragedy in the public sphere.

The period subsequent to the murder demonstrated Jackie's ability to persevere in the midst of emotional devastation. The individual had an exceptional capacity to manage her own personal sorrow with the shared grieving process experienced by a whole country. The display of her fortitude was evident throughout the state burial, as seen by her controlled manner and her selection of clothes, including the classic black veil and coat, which further emphasized her dignity.

The visual depiction of her accompanying her spouse's coffin, accompanied by her children, became indelibly imprinted on the communal consciousness as a profound symbol of bereavement and fortitude.

The last years of Jackie's life were characterized by a phase of self-reflection and personal growth. The individual actively sought emotional support and a sense of safety, deriving consolation from seclusion as they navigated the many challenges associated with their experience of loss. The widow's responsibilities, in conjunction with her position as a prominent figure, necessitated her to carefully navigate the intersection of personal recovery and societal demands. Notwithstanding the obstacles encountered, she successfully reconfigured her sense of self in a manner that acknowledged and respected historical influences, while simultaneously embracing the potentialities that lie ahead.

In the year 1968, Jacqueline Kennedy Onassis garnered significant media attention via her marriage with Aristotle Onassis, a prominent figure in the Greek shipping industry. The actions of the union were met with astonishment and perplexity, leading to the initiation of debates and discussions about its underlying intentions and the potential ramifications on its legacy. Although there were some who raised doubts about her choice, it is important to analyze it within the context of her own trajectory. The association she had with Onassis afforded her company and a feeling of security, enabling her to effectively negotiate the intricacies of her altered circumstances.

During this particular phase, Jackie experienced a time of relative solitude, as she withdrew from public scrutiny. In an effort to evade the intrusive gaze of the media, she sought sanctuary on Skorpios, the private island owned by Onassis. During this period, she was afforded the opportunity to recuperate, engage in introspection, and regain her own identity. In spite of the difficulties and critical examination of her recent marriage, she exemplified the intricate and highly individual nature of personal choices, which are frequently shaped by a variety of reasons extending outside the realm of public observation.

After the demise of Onassis in 1975, Jackie's reentry into the United States signified yet another pivotal moment. The individual reignited her fervor for literature and the arts, fully engaging herself in a professional pursuit within the publishing industry. This undertaking served as evidence of her diverse range of abilities, demonstrating her capacity to actively participate in intellectual discourse and make valuable contributions to the cultural sphere.

Jackie's professional trajectory in the field of editorial work included employment at many publishing establishments, including Viking Press and Doubleday. She used her influential position to provide assistance to up-and-coming writers and advocate for literary works that aligned with her intellectual and aesthetic preferences. Her venture into the realm of publishing afforded her an opportunity to establish a platform for engaging with authors, artists, and intellectuals, therefore making a lasting impact on the literary sphere.

Moreover, her engagement in charitable endeavors persisted in emphasizing her dedication to the advancement of culture and education. The individual in question held positions on the governing bodies of renowned institutions such as the Metropolitan Museum of Art and the John F. Kennedy Center for the Performing Arts, so contributing to her lasting reputation as a supporter of artistic endeavors. The aforementioned positions exemplified her unwavering commitment to cultivating innovation, safeguarding cultural legacy, and developing the aptitudes of forthcoming cohorts.

During the last stages of her life, Jackie consistently shown tenacity and maintained a sense of enduring elegance. The narrative of her life included a series of adversities, individual obstacles, and profound encounters that depicted a lady who consistently underwent personal growth while remaining steadfast in her fundamental principles. The ongoing evidence to her effect on American culture and beyond is evident via her legacy as a cultural icon, champion for historical preservation, and patron of the arts.

In conclusion, the latter life of Jackie Kennedy serves as a tribute to her exceptional perseverance and adeptness in navigating the intricacies of life. She demonstrated the ability of the human spirit to triumph through hardship, transitioning from profound sorrow to profound personal growth. The decisions made by the individual in question, although being subject to critical examination, served as a manifestation of her own trajectory, so serving as a poignant reminder that the routes we traverse are often influenced by many factors and our own development. In her final years, she exemplified the capacity to discover significance, purpose, and a revitalized self amidst adversity.

CHAPTER 7

Philanthropic Activities

The legacy of Jackie Kennedy beyond her status as a fashion star and First Lady, including her philanthropic endeavors that reflect her unwavering commitment to effecting good change in society. The individual's charitable endeavors, distinguished by a sincere ardor for the arts, education, and cultural enhancement, have had a lasting impact on American society and continue to serve as a source of inspiration for subsequent generations.

Jackie's engagement in philanthropic endeavors was firmly grounded in her profound admiration for the arts and her conviction in their capacity to effect profound change. The individual saw that the arts had a significance beyond personal gratification, as they possessed the capacity to cultivate comprehension, bridge disparities, and enhance the human condition. The aforementioned comprehension was readily apparent via her substantial engagement with cultural establishments, enabling her to advocate for the utilization of the arts as means for educational advancement, personal development, and societal advancement.

Jackie made a notable contribution to the arts mostly via her affiliation with the Metropolitan Museum of Art. In her capacity as a board member of the museum, she significantly contributed to advancing its objective of preserving and exhibiting a diverse array of global cultural masterpieces. The individual's presence and impact played a vital role in garnering interest towards the museum's exhibits and collections, therefore fostering a wider audience's involvement in and admiration for art originating from other cultures and historical eras.

Jackie's dedication to the performing arts was shown via her active participation with the John F. Kennedy Center for the Performing Arts. The center was established as a tribute to her deceased spouse, serving as a representation of Jackie's commitment to fostering creative creativity and facilitating cultural interchange. In her capacity as a board trustee, she demonstrated unwavering dedication towards the fulfillment of the center's objective, which included the facilitation of artistic expression, the cultivation of creativity, and the promotion of widespread accessibility to the arts.

In addition to her contributions to the artistic world, she also engaged in charity endeavors related to education. Acknowledging the significance of cultivating the intellectual development of young individuals and cultivating a passion for acquiring knowledge, she campaigned for efforts aimed at advancing education and developing intellectual maturation. Jackie comprehended the pivotal role of education in advancing society, and she used her influential position to advocate for initiatives that fostered personal growth and enabled people to achieve their utmost capabilities.

One of her noteworthy educational endeavors is the foundation of the Jacqueline Kennedy Onassis Award for

Outstanding Public Service Benefiting Disadvantaged Urban Areas. The award acknowledges people and organizations that have made noteworthy contributions to urban neighborhoods through means of education, community development, and social empowerment. Through highlighting these initiatives, Jackie aimed to promote more investment in education and community development within marginalized regions.

Moreover, her engagement in the arts and education was congruent with her fervor for the conservation of historical heritage. The individual's dedication to the conservation of historical elements extended beyond architectural structures and notable sites. They recognized the need of maintaining cultural heritage by also preserving the creative manifestations of earlier eras. By means of her charitable endeavors, she advocated for programs that safeguarded the preservation of creative artifacts and the narratives they encapsulated.

Jackie's philanthropic approach exhibited a profound level of personal involvement and direct engagement. She did not only provide her name in support of various causes, but rather actively participated in organizations, events, and interactions with people, using her power to bring about beneficial transformations. The individual's capacity to establish meaningful connections with others from many backgrounds, in conjunction with her authentic display of empathy, made her a proficient champion for the issues she really valued.

In a society that often prioritizes material riches and celebrity status, Jackie's charity pursuits serve as a poignant reminder of the profound impact that altruism can have. The donations made by her extended beyond mere financial assistance. They served as evidence of her firm conviction in the capacity of the arts, education, and cultural preservation to uplift society and enhance the quality of life. The enduring impact of her legacy serves as a source of inspiration for philanthropists, artists, educators, and others who want to use their power in order to promote societal progress.

In summary, the charitable endeavors undertaken by Jackie Kennedy serve as evidence of her deep-seated conviction about the significance of the arts, education, and the preservation of cultural heritage. The individual's unwavering support for renowned cultural establishments such as the Metropolitan Museum of Art and the John F. Kennedy Center for the Performing Arts exemplified her steadfast devotion to cultivating creativity and promoting the manifestation of creative ideas.

THE END

Milton Keynes UK
Ingram Content Group UK Ltd.
UKHW020730220923
429186UK00015B/901